ETERNAL ROOTS

Who Am I and Why Am I Here?

The answer to the question "Who am I?" comes not from self-analysis but through personal commitment...it is the landmark decision of life outside of which nothing has value and inside of which every relationship and achievement, every success and failure, derives its meaning. It deals a mortal blow to cynicism, self-hatred, and despair." Abba's Father, P. 160, by Brennan Manning.

3/19/2020
Biblemapsplus.com
Maralyn B. Dyck

ACKNOWLEDGEMENTS

I wish to thank all those who read my book and helped with suggestions and corrections.

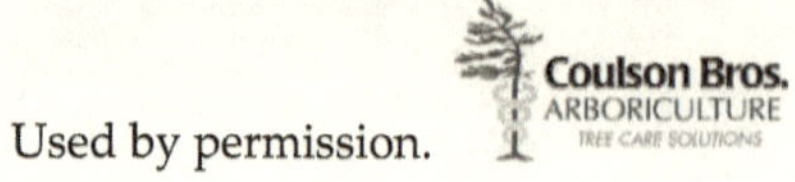

Used by permission.

ISBN: 9798628833469

COPYRIGHT 2020 © Maralyn B. Dyck - March, 2020

Table of Contents

FACTS YOU NEED TO KNOW BEFORE YOU READ THIS BOOK!

1 Empty space is exactly that...empty space...no energy, no particles.

2 It is impossible for empty space to evolve into something, empty means just that...empty! No evolution!

3 Eternal or Eternity is endless, no beginning, no middle and no ending.

4 There has to be an Intelligent Being that is also without beginning, exists now and always will exist!

5 Everything that now exists, the universes, trillions of them, including Earth and our universal system, do have a beginning.

6 This Intelligent Being has many names, but the Name that we know is GOD. There is a God.

7 God has no beginning and no ending; He is eternal, omniscient, omnipotent, omnipresent, sovereign, and unchangeable. You cannot hide from God!

8 There is only ONE TRUE GOD!

If you understand the above statements, enjoy the book and learn more about yourself, your roots and your destiny!

CHAPTER ONE

"And he will be [nourished] like a tree planted by the waters,
That spreads out its roots by the river;
And will not fear the heat when it comes;
But its leaves will be green and moist.
And it will not be anxious and concerned in a year of drought
Nor stop bearing fruit." Jeremiah 17:8

In Revelation 22:1, John says, "He showed me a river of the water of life, clear as crystal, coming from the throne of God and of the Lamb..." This "water of life" for us is found in God's Word, the Holy Bible. Above, Jeremiah tells us that we are to be like a tree planted by the waters, spreading out our roots to be nourished by the pure waters running past our bank.

If our roots are firmly planted on the bank of the river, we can be strong enough and healthy enough to withstand all the storms and problems of life that come our way. We will bear fruit and will be able to fulfill God's Plan A for our life.

God knows we cannot do this on our own and we will make many mistakes, but He has also provided a way for us to be renewed and transplanted on the bank of the waters of life for eternity, even while still here on earth. It does not depend on our perfection or our terrible background, which may contain many horrible deeds or failures. NO sin is too great for God to forgive.

This book is a study of our roots, our story and our actions. It will help you to determine where you are in life, Plans A+ through F, how to deal with your situation where you are and to learn the wonderful truths that are provided by God for those seeking to know Him and change their lives forever. Your destiny is in your hands, it's your choice. Join me now as we travel this journey together. Be honest with yourself when grading your status; no one will see your results, just you and God.

WHO AM I? – In the beginning...Genesis 1:1-3

Before the six days of creation of the earth and all that is upon it there was a great rebellion in heaven by Satan (a powerful archangel of God), and one-third of the angels joined in his rebellion. They wanted to rule heaven and have great power.

[7]"And war broke out in heaven, Michael [the archangel] and his angels waging war with the dragon. The dragon (Satan) and the angels fought,

8but they were not strong enough and did not prevail, and there was no longer a place found for them in heaven.

9And the great dragon was thrown down, the age-old serpent who is called the devil and Satan, he who *continually* deceives *and* seduces the entire inhabited world; he was thrown down to the earth, and his angels were thrown down with him. Revelation 12:7-9

God could not allow that, so Satan and his "fallen angels" were removed from heaven and sent down to live in the bowels of the earth. God created a lake of fire there called Hell. This Hell was created as the home for Satan and the fallen angels, not for human beings! Human beings go there by choice when they side with Satan. Their actual dominion would include the surface of the whole earth. The precise timing of this event is not given, but most likely would be before the creation of Adam and Eve; Satan caused their fall by using the snake that spoke to Eve. Some day we will know. It does not matter; the facts are that Satan and his angels are on earth and have created havoc ever since and will do so until the end of time.

Luke also refers to the above event; "He (Jesus) said to them (his 77 followers at that time), "I watched Satan fall from heaven like [a flash of] lightning. Listen carefully: I have given you authority [that you now possess] to tread on serpents and scorpions, and [the ability to exercise that authority] over all the power of the enemy (Satan); and nothing will [in any way] harm you......" Luke 10:18-19

On the sixth day of creation the first man and woman were created and entered a beautiful perfect world. They were without sin; they were spiritual beings.

Genesis 1:26: "Let Us (Father, Son, Holy Spirit) make man in Our image, according to <u>Our likeness</u> [not physical, but a spiritual personality and moral likeness;] and let them have complete authority over the fish of the sea, the birds of the air, the cattle, and over the entire earth, and over everything that creeps *and* crawls on the earth."They did so.

God created Adam, from the dust of the ground, in His own image and likeness, a spiritual being; He put Adam to sleep and removed a rib to form a woman. A woman was born of a man, to be his companion. Adam called her Eve. God planted a garden for them and called it Eden. He placed them in the garden to care for it. In those days there was no rain, but a mist rose from the ground to water the entire surface of the earth. Read Genesis 1:1-3 for the full story.

They are the first ancestors of ALL of us, our first DNA! They lived in perfection in Plan A+, the perfect life in tune with their Creator. How did we get to where we are now? We have a life of sorrow and illness, tragedy and wars. There are good times; but what happened to change us, causing us to lose life in the Garden of Eden? *Sin happened.*

God gave them all of the trees and vegetables of the garden to eat forever, *on one condition.* They could eat of all the fruit of the trees in the garden, except for one specific tree located in the middle of the garden. Its name was "the tree of the knowledge of good and evil." He told them that the day they ate of that tree, they would die (would be separated from God, a spiritual death, immediately, followed later by physical death).

To make a long story short, Adam and Eve ate some of the forbidden fruit after the snake, controlled by Satan, deceived Eve. Eve gave some to Adam and he ate as well, knowing that he was disobeying God. God could not tolerate sin [disobedience] in Eden, so he removed both of them outside of Eden where they possibly lived in caves which were and still are, plentiful. Read Genesis 3 for all of the details. Their story belongs in this book as *they are our first ancestors*!

God did not want robots serving Him day and night; He wanted a people who would be willing and delighted to serve Him. He gave them freedom of choice and that choice still exists until this day. They chose to disobey and they died spiritually immediately and were placed outside the garden of Eden. Physical death came many years later after giving birth to many descendants.

What actually happened here? Sin entered the world. Now every human being is born "in sin." This means that we no longer are spiritually perfect people. We are severed from God and will stay that way unless we personally make a choice to serve Him, accepting Jesus Christ as our personal Savior.

If you are an unbeliever or are not sure of your position with God at this point, I would recommend that you go to the last chapter of this book called, "God's Plan for Your Life." It will give you an introduction to becoming a believer. You may even decide to become one before you continue with this next part of the book.

TYPES OF ROOTS – Stage One: In this chapter we will determine your actual generational roots in each of 4 categories:
1 – Ethnic Background: races or peoples as distinguished by speech, customs and characteristics.
2 – Religious Background: There could be more than one.
3 – Medical Background: Known illnesses and health issues in the past. This includes cause of death, medical or accident, etc.
4 – Cultural Background-Customs and activities, such as business people, farmers, miners, teachers, etc.

1 – **Ethnic background**. If you know it, list your ancestral background here or on a separate piece of paper.

____

____

____

____

Your ancestors may be from one or more countries; it helps to know these countries as they can provide clues to what you may have inherited in your genes.

It can give you an idea as to why you think various thoughts, some of your actions and even some of your desires. Every person is born with different roots and each person is very special and unique in the eyes of God. We do not control our first roots, but we need to understand them, accept them and go forward.

****

Did you realize that every human being is an *eternal being*, a person without a beginning and without an ending? In the Bible when God was speaking to Jeremiah, He said, "*Before* I formed you in the womb *I knew you...*" Jeremiah 1:5

****

We **will** have eternal life, eternal life in heaven with God **or** eternal life in the lake of fire with Satan. It is our choice. *No death, ever*! You cannot escape from God; earthly death is ETERNAL LIFE in either the lake of fire or heaven! Choose wisely.

Never despise or think badly of your ethnic background; God knows all about it. God loves variety! Can you imagine what the world would be like if we all looked exactly the same. We would be robots! What a boring way to be.

He chose what our ethnic background would be from the very beginning! He knows all about us, even what choices we will make. God does not want robots; He wants people who want Him, want to serve Him and worship Him. He has given us the freedom of choice. We will discuss this aspect in more detail later in the book.

If you are not sure of your DNA, just do the best you can to analyze what background you have from what you do know. This is not an exam! It will be very helpful to know about your DNA roots, if you discover them.

Why is this important? In some cases there are **generational** roots with which we have to deal in our own life. We need to gather all the facts of our initial roots before we discuss what it means and what to do with the results we discover. DNA test kits are very inexpensive and are available at your local drug store. Take a swab of your saliva and mail it in. They will test it and send you the results.

2 – **Religious background**. If there is more than one, list all of them and, if known, how devout and faithful were your ancestors – casual, fairly devout or extremely involved. Which faith was the strongest in the latest ones, such as parents and grandparents. It does make a great difference overall on how you are affected by this background.

Remember, this is BEFORE conception. We will also deal with the current effects as they affect our lives during the course of this book.

____

____

____

3 – **Medical background**. List all the known ones that you can discover. They can help to determine, even years later, why you

have various health problems and where your health may be at risk, just from generational sources.

____

____

____

____

4 – **Cultural background**. This would deal with the occupations of various families and the activities in which they liked to participate. Some of this can also filter down to show up in your own likes and dislikes. It will not define who you are, but will help you to understand at times why you like some things and not others and as they most likely have some affect on what you choose to be when you grow up. Write these down on your list as well.

____

____

____

____

Once you have had time to digest all this information, remember it, as we progress into the following chapters. You will know when to refer back to them by the topics being discussed.

The first roots are inherited and that will not change. How we deal with them will make a difference as we travel through our life experiences.

These are normal roots from conception to birth. Can be twisted and knurled depending upon what happens to the mother during her pregnancy.

Type of Roots – Stage Two:

This section will take us from conception to birth. The roots grow and change even while you are in your mother's womb! New characteristics, both good and not so good, will affect you, depending on what happens in your mother's life! During the months of pregnancy, a baby's personality begins to develop!

A calm and peaceful pregnancy can produce a happy baby with not a care in the world; a harsh and angry pregnancy can produce a baby that cries a lot and even appears to have temper tantrums! They just "learn" from what they hear and sense from what is happening in the mother's life. A depressed mother can give birth to a baby who fights depression very early in life.

Many years ago I heard a testimony that has stayed with me all these years. Yes, testimonies are important! Be sure to share experiences with others; they do have an impact and can be very important to someone else.

When this girl was very little, about three years old, she started humming a tune. The mother, recognizing the tune was startled! She had not heard that tune since her little girl was born. She sang it to her many times during her pregnancy, but not since her birth. She waited until she finished singing the tune and asked her where she had heard it. She did not seem to know.

She asked her husband and he did not know the song himself. The only place she could have heard it, and often, was when she was in her mother's womb! She sang it to her while she rocked her to sleep! It was not a current tune but one that her own mother had taught her when she was little! What a wonderful inheritance for that child.

Compare that to a child that seems unhappy and angry even while very young. Perhaps the parents were fighting, depressed or troubled during the baby's pregnancy period. It is important to keep close to God during this time in order to provide a wonderful inheritance for the child once they are born.

How did all our troubles begin? Remember the story of Adam and Eve? When Adam and Eve disobeyed God's command, God placed them outside Eden and cursed the land and all His creations because of this sin. Sin entered the world and had to be dealt with immediately. God could not tolerate any sin in His kingdom or in Eden.

As a result we are ALL born in sin. The Bible clearly states that there is none righteous, not even one! Salvation for babies is not automatic. That is one reason, among others, that Christians dedicate their children to God as babies. They have not yet reached the age of accountability. They are covered by their parents until they understand right from wrong, and it is up to the parents to teach them early about Jesus and their need to personally accept Him as their Savior.

To us this may seem harsh, but God has extremely high standards for His people. Hear what Apostle Paul had to say:

10b"There is none righteous [none that meets God's standard], not even one.
11There is none who understands,
there is none who seeks for God.
12All have turned aside, together
they have become useless; there is none who
does good, no, not one." Romans 3:10b-12

When babies reach the age of accountability, it becomes their choice to make the decision to serve Jesus. Christian parents should make sure their children hear the word of God and how Jesus loves them from the time they are VERY little, even if they take a while to understand what is being said.

I believe they are covered by their parents until they reach the age of accountability, whenever God determines that to be. Adopted children would also be covered by praying parents. Babies born to ungodly parents would not be covered by praying parents. This is my belief; you do not have to agree with me to understand what you are as a person.

Remember, we are born in sin; at that stage we are sinners. It is okay if you disagree with me; you have the right to your own thoughts on this subject. However, you need to start teaching your children about Jesus right from birth, songs at first and short Bible stories when they are a bit older. Teach them how to pray and teach them the difference between right and wrong.

Let them make their own spiritual choices. Forcing them will drive them away. Just encourage them and love them when they go astray, and most children will, even for a short while, if not seriously in trouble. Love them and make sure they know it. They will not forget in the long run. Pray without ceasing; that is one secret for good parenting.

Do not slap them, shake them or get angry—easier said than done, but necessary, if you wish to keep them in the long run. Try using restrictions, rather than beatings: i.e. confiscate cell phones, cut allowance for a time, no television for a time. Curfews and extra chores sometimes work for older ones.

Each child is different; make sure they KNOW they are loved and appreciated even when being disciplined. Hard? Of course it is. Life is not easy. Hug your children often; they need constant reassurance that they are loved and needed.

All of the above statements are just to say that life can start rough or easy depending on how our mother acts, whether she has terrible trauma in her life, emotional upsets, depression, excitement, illness, accident, you name it; it can all affect what we become at the time of our birth. If our mother was a drug addict or an alcoholic, this could cause medical problems for us.

Premature birth due to accident, illness or mistreatment will also affect our health and well-being at the time of our birth. However, God knows all about that, so leave the future to Him. First, we learn what it has all been like in our past, and then we can figure out where we are and what, if anything, we need to do to rectify the situation. Knowing these facts will help us judge our thoughts and actions throughout the years of our life.

Some people do not know or have access to any of this information. Sometimes we have to figure some of it out as we go. If you have a dark outlook on life, perhaps things were not so good during pregnancy. If you have a happy outgoing personality, then you may have had a good and safe beginning.

Current medical issues could relate to inherited tendencies. These are gauges in learning to understand ourselves and, possibly, where we were at this particular stage of our development. Only we can judge more accurately about ourselves. We are still held responsible for our own actions.

What we are attempting to do at this stage is to get a sense of where our actions and thoughts come from at this point in time. We really need to give some serious thought to what we do know about ourselves, and then we can move forward.

These first two stages provide the beginning of the root system of our life, the "tree" that needs to be planted on the river bank. These early stages will be for discussion after birth.

Up to this point there is complete innocence on the part of the child. While born in sin, a baby has not committed any sins of its own yet. These early roots are not in our control. We just need to understand what they are.

Some of the roots during pregnancy are damaged, but many of the roots can be straightened, strengthened, weakened or even destroyed, by what follows in successive areas of our lives; you will not always be responsible for what happens.

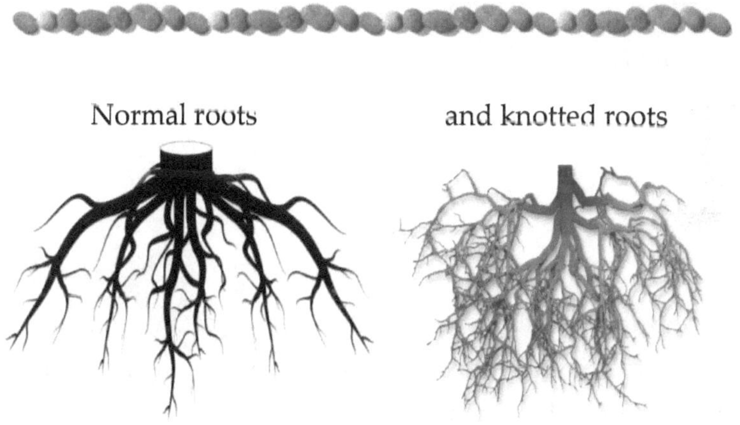

Normal roots   and knotted roots

TYPE OF ROOTS – Phase Three:

At birth your roots have not yet been planted anywhere other than in your mother. Now life begins and activities once again change your roots. They can become strengthened or twisted, shrivelled up, or badly damaged by what happens during your childhood. OR, they can be strengthened and nourished and grow strong all the way through to old age.

As young people become older and begin their adult life, many spread out all over the earth and choose to dwell in all types of places and climates. The same type of activity happens to our spiritual lives, changing our roots.

We can live in the desert enjoying life for a spell, but if there is no water, even that type of life cannot exist for long. The roots will dry up and wither away. Water is essential to life.

Mountainous areas can be challenging and even fun, but if there are too many rocks, our roots will wither away even here for lack of soil and water. Life is in the soil and nourishment is in the water. Both are necessary for a healthy development of both our physical bodies and our spiritual bodies—our spiritual heart.

Our spiritual hearts are like a garden. We have soil in our heart to nourish the seed, but what type of soil and what type of seed are we planting in that garden? Do we have soft healthy soil, or sand, or rocks, or weeds? What about the seed? Are we sowing seeds of evil or good seeds? Are we removing weeds on a daily basis (asking forgiveness) or allowing a wild garden that is out of control? We need the help of God's Holy Spirit to guide us and help us produce a good crop and a beautiful garden (soul and spirit).

The health, condition and strength of our garden will determine how well we face the terrible storms and bad weather of life that can tear our roots from the ground, almost destroying our lives. Strong, deep roots will survive any storm that we face. These roots are planted firmly on the banks of the river of life where God transplants new believers upon salvation.

Some families survive the storms of life and live wholesome lives. However, their "fruit," for many, is scarce and sometimes does not bear fruit in its season.

There is only one place in the whole world where your "tree" needs to be, on the banks of the river of life. There it can flourish and produce fruit in its season and the roots will grow strong and straight, drinking from the water of life day and night! *Now it is time to grow leaves and bear fruit!*

By now I probably have some of you completely confused. We need to collect more details to which you can relate.

Psalm 1:2-3: "But His delight is in the law of the Lord, and on His law [His precepts and teachings] he [habitually} meditates day and night. And he will be like a tree *firmly* planted [and fed] by streams of water, which yields its fruit in its season; its leaf does not wither; and whatever he does, he prospers [and comes to maturity].

Revelation 22:1-2: "Then the angel showed me a river of the water of life, clear as crystal, flowing from the throne of God and of the Lamb (Christ), in the middle of the street. On either side of the river was the tree of life, bearing twelve *kinds of* fruit, yielding its fruit every month; and the leaves of the tree were for the healing of the nations."

Our goal here on earth is to bear the fruits of the Holy Spirit and also to bear the "fruit" of the womb, our babies that God gives us. For those who do not or cannot bear children physically they can still bear new believers for God, spiritual children. We can also enjoy and help with children that are already amongst us, in the neighbourhood or church. God promises that the barren woman will have a quiver full; this can mean adopted children or spiritual children, of any age.

God is good and does not leave any of us out. We can all reach God's Plan A for our lives...our choice depends on how much we want to be with Jesus and how much time we are willing to give Him in prayer and worship, over and above our daily living. Plan A+ is heaven and none of us are ready to be there yet!

The next page shows the four plans as represented by the growth of trees. Refer back to page 24 from time to time as you read through the book and try to determine where you are at the time and decide where you want to be for the rest of your life.

Trees have to be constantly watered and nourished to grow to be beautiful and productive. An explanation about all of this is provided in this book. Remember: you only need to know this so that you know where to begin making changes in your lifestyle to get where you want to be. Jesus Christ is the answer and the Holy Bible is your teacher with the assistance of the Holy Spirit. Do not be discouraged; all this will be described more fully as you read the following pages.

D's Agnostics

C's Nominal unbelievers

B's New and Average believers

A's Strong and active believers

This picture depicts roots as they develop under the surface of the soil. Roots are affected by everything that we do in our lives.

EARLY CHILDHOOD – Up to the age of accountability

The age of accountability is different for each child and depends on their ability to understand right from wrong. This can be very early for some, later for others. Only God knows their hearts and how much they understand.

Some children have the advantage of a wonderful Christian home and understand at a very early age who Jesus is and that they need to be obedient to parents, kind to others and willing to share their toys. They may not understand the full impact that the environment has on their development, but that comes with growing older.

Some experts have been quoted as saying that the most impactful time of a person's life is during the first seven years!

Children are very vulnerable during this period of time, for their understanding is only beginning to develop and grow.

They are learning many new things every day and most of the time they are not even aware that they are learning anything. They just live.

Unfortunately, some children are not "raised" at all. Their homes are a disaster; their parents are drug addicts, alcoholics, criminals and some are never around when they are needed.

These children take care of themselves and many turn out like their parents, down and out, and in all kinds of trouble and despair. Their little roots are twisted and damaged, some beyond natural repair, others are changed through life experiences later in their lives.

In the middle area are children in all kinds of circumstances; good, bad and the ugly. There is a blend of all of these for others. However, do not despair. No matter how bad your upbringing during these early years, you can still have a wonderful and fulfilling life.

God knows what your childhood years
were like, but He loves you just the same. "For God
so [greatly] loved the world *and* that He [even]
gave His [one and] only begotten Son, so that
whoever believes *and* **trusts** in Him [as Savior]
shall not perish, but have eternal life." John 3:16.

For this chapter you will need your pencil again to continue with the analysis of yourself.

For this first part jot down in outline form what you remember from your childhood days up to seven years old. If you remember any thoughts or questions you had unanswered at the time, jot those down as well. Be honest with yourself. You are the only one who will be looking at what you write. You might get some answers as you continue reading.

____

____

____

____

____

____

____

In the following list, put a check mark on one choice, 1 being the worst or none and 5 the best or many. Some questions require listed responses.

SCHOOL YEARS - Age 6 through all school years, including college.

How do you rate your school years? 1___ 2___ 3___ 4___ 5__
How would you rate College?   1___ 2___ 3___ 4___ 5__

Briefly list anything that actually traumatized or blessed you. Include any experience, bad and good, that you will never forget.

____

____

____

____

____

____

____

____

Think carefully about this time of your life. These experiences will all have a bearing on what happens in your adult years.

Were you ever a bully?	1___ 2___ 3___ 4___ 5___
Did you have any special friends?	1___ 2___ 3___ 4___ 5___
Were you mean or cranky?	1___ 2___ 3___ 4___ 5___
Are you pleasant to be around?	1___ 2___ 3___ 4___ 5___
Did enjoy school? Why?	1___ 2___ 3___ 4___ 5___

____

____

____

Get to know yourself during those years. There is no "correct" answer. Include college in this section. Include any technical training or degrees you obtained.

____

____

____

____

Did you get involved in drugs, drinking, or sexual activities outside of marriage?	1___ 2___ 3___ 4___ 5___

Did you participate in any criminal
  activities?   1__ 2__ 3__ 4__ 5__
Did you tell lies, gossip or exaggerate
  to get what you wanted?   1__ 2__ 3__ 4__ 5__
Have you ever been guilty of conning
  people out of money?   1__ 2__ 3__ 4__ 5__
Rate your employment situations.   1__ 2__ 3__ 4__ 5__
Did you follow a career?   1__ 2__ 3__ 4__ 5__
If married, have you been faithful and
  loving to your spouse? Children? 1__ 2__ 3__ 4__ 5__
Did you ignore your family in order
  to climb the financial ladder?   1__ 2__ 3__ 4__ 5__
Were you ever controlling, mean, or
  unforgiving in any degree?   1__ 2__ 3__ 4__ 5__
Did you help others in distress?   1__ 2__ 3__ 4__ 5__
Were you generous with your time? 1__ 2__ 3__ 4__ 5__
Your attitude towards others?   1__ 2__ 3__ 4__ 5__
Put others first when appropriate? 1__ 2__ 3__ 4__ 5__
Are you keeping to yourself?   1__ 2__ 3__ 4__ 5__
Do you feel sorry for yourself
  when negative things happen?   1__ 2__ 3__ 4__ 5__
Do you deal with situations and
go on?   1__ 2__ 3__ 4__ 5__
Are you cheerful in nature?   1__ 2__ 3__ 4__ 5__
Disinterested in life as a whole?   1__ 2__ 3__ 4__ 5__
Are you a workalcoholic?   1__ 2__ 3__ 4__ 5__
Are you forgiving and gentle?   1__ 2__ 3__ 4__ 5__
Do you act gruff or anger easily?   1__ 2__ 3__ 4__ 5__
Your level of care about others?   1__ 2__ 3__ 4__ 5__

Are you protective of your rights and
when they conflict with others?   1___ 2___ 3___ 4___ 5___
Are you willing to negotiate and
compromise?   1___ 2___ 3___ 4___ 5___
Do you like to party?   1___ 2___ 3___ 4___ 5___
Do you prefer to be alone, doing
your own thing?   1___ 2___ 3___ 4___ 5___
Are you comfortable in a crowd?   1___ 2___ 3___ 4___ 5___
Are you interested in any sports?   1___ 2___ 3___ 4___ 5___
Do you participate in any sports?   1___ 2___ 3___ 4___ 5___
How serious are you about sports?   1___ 2___ 3___ 4___ 5___
Amount of time watching sports?   1___ 2___ 3___ 4___ 5___
Do you get upset when you lose?   1___ 2___ 3___ 4___ 5___
Do you brag when you win?   1___ 2___ 3___ 4___ 5___
Amount of time spent chatting on
your phone or computer?   1___ 2___ 3___ 4___ 5___
Do you play games on the computer? 1___ 2___ 3___ 4___ 5___
Do you do business online?   1___ 2___ 3___ 4___ 5___
Do you spend prime time with your
family or close friends?   1___ 2___ 3___ 4___ 5___
Do you make an effort to create new
friendships?   1___ 2___ 3___ 4___ 5___
Do you like to read?   1___ 2___ 3___ 4___ 5___
How much time do you spend reading?1___ 2___ 3___ 4___ 5___
What type of books do you like to read?

____

____

____

____

This can also give you clues as to what is going on in your life. Some people live in a fantasy world, just so that they can escape dealing with the real one! It can also be an escape from boredom or fill in time when you are tired or not feeling well.

The type of books you read can also give you a glimpse into what you are and can help you determine the proper balance between reading and other things that you could be doing. For some it is seeking knowledge and wisdom which is a very healthy and a worthwhile activity.

How much time do you spend on
  crafts or hobbies?   1___ 2___ 3___ 4___ 5___
Do you share them with others?   1___ 2___ 3___ 4___ 5___
Do you sell any of them for profit? 1___ 2___ 3___ 4___ 5___

Time management – this topic can open your eyes to what is really going on in your life! Analyze how you spend your time; when, where and for how long.

Time spent for personal things?   1___ 2___ 3___ 4___ 5___
Allowing time for others?   1___ 2___ 3___ 4___ 5___

Hobbies are very good but they can be a crutch to make you feel good about yourself just because you may be feeling lost and hopeless in other situations. On the other hand they can be very therapeutic, depending on your particular needs and interests. They can also be very productive and worthwhile.

A well planned lifestyle can also improve your attitude towards yourself and others. I am not referring to a rigid time-related schedule. Rather, I am referring to a **balance** between activities and reality, things that **must** be done, and what you like to do.

Are you always in a hurry?	1___ 2___ 3___ 4___ 5___
Are you habitually late?	1___ 2___ 3___ 4___ 5___
Unorganized in your activities?	1___ 2___ 3___ 4___ 5___

You need to slow down, take a deep breath, and do some deep thinking about how you can change bad habits into good ones. You will soon feel much better about yourself when you straighten out your life a bit. Depression and misery keep the disorganized person out of sync with the world around them, making them even more miserable.

Think about the jobs or careers that you have had over the years, both full time and part time. Were any of them fulfilling? On an average did you feel successful, okay or like a miserable failure?   1___ 2___ 3___ 4___ 5___

These emotions happen to everyone at one point or another. How you feel about yourself will color all future attempts to work or start a new career. You can feel confident or fearful. There is a verse I read that really fits in with this situation.

"What I always feared has happened to me.
What I dreaded has come true."Job 3:25 NLT

What you fear will come upon you! This often happens in life. You are afraid of getting cancer and, down the road, you get cancer! This is just one example. If you stop to think about it carefully, you may come up with many other examples to justify this statement. A **positive attitude** helps to work wonders. A positive attitude helps to avoid depression or discouragement.

There are "triggers" for every aspect of your life; triggers that make you happy, make you sad, make you angry, make you jealous, make you spiteful and so on. Learn your triggers and work to make the bad ones less damaging to both yourself and others.

Coping with a triggered action *must not be immediate*. Control yourself and act the way you should during any given situation. Do not give in to the triggers. Even good triggers can get out of control. **Balance** is crucial. List your triggers and reactions to them.

____

____

____

____

____

____

____

____

What are your personal hopes and dreams?

____

____

____

Do you have a goal for your life?

____

____

Without dreams and goals, life will become boring and meaningless. Dreams and goals will help to keep you focused and happy as you face all of life's unexpected events and challenges. Start by deciding on your first goal, a small one to begin, one that is within your current ability.

Once accomplished begin to get larger goals and maybe even a long term goal. They can change, but at least they give you something to look forward to and provide focus, prevent depression and discouragement. Failed? Try a different goal. NEVER give up, that always leads to failure and discouragement.

Many years ago I was told that if I fell off a horse, I should get back on right away and try again and again. It works. You will discover how much better you feel about yourself when you keep getting up again. It also helps to deter fear of falling again.

Family relationships and relationships with other people need to be nourished and cherished. The time may come when you will need them by your side! Do unto others as you would have them do to you – a famous quote and very true. Do NOT shut yourself out from anyone, especially your family and close friends. You all need each other. **God did not make us to live alone and lonely.** We are to be a part of a local community. This should include relatives, neighbors and a sound local church.

We all need to know God and grow spiritually; attending a church regularly and participating in church activities can help us grow spiritually as well as mentally. These people can become closer than a family in some cases, caring for you when needed, and you caring for them. Try to befriend even the unlovely and street people where possible. You might be surprised at the results down the road! Even a smile can go a long ways!

Physical disabilities can also hamper us, but it does not need to make us an unhappy or a useless person. Our attitude will make all the difference in how we see ourselves and how others will respond and act towards us. Now is a good time to go back to your roots starting with conception.

Compare what you wrote during those questions to what you have become since and see where, if possible, how your current personality, likes and dislikes actually began before you were born! You may find similarities between yourself and some of your ancestors. I think you will understand that some of your behaviour in later years, both good and bad, had a firm beginning in all of your original roots.

DEALING WITH GENERATIONAL ROOTS

Generational roots can affect our lives today! They need to be dealt with as soon as possible. What am I talking about? Let's start with God's perspective:

Exodus 20:5: "...for I, the Lord your God, am a jealous (impassioned) God [demanding what is rightfully and uniquely mine], visiting (avenging) the iniquity (sin, guilt) of the fathers on the children [that is, calling the children to account for the sins of their fathers], to the third and fourth generations of those who hate Me..."
(See also: Deuteronomy 5:9-10; Jeremiah 32:17-18)

What does this mean? If your ancestors were ungodly, you have inherited an ungodly lineage. This is not a problem and can be easily dealt with by talking to God and giving your life to Jesus! When you do this, ask God to forgive the sins of your ancestors that has impacted your life. It is that simple.

However, if Satanism, in any form, was involved, ask Jesus to cast out any demonic activity, activated by your ancestors, out of your life and back to Hell where they belong. The blood of Jesus covers ALL sins and demons cannot stay; they have to go.

That said, demons will be more likely to continue trying to get back into your life because of your heritage, but Jesus is the answer. Keep close to Jesus and you will have nothing to fear. They look for weak spots in your spiritual walk to attack you again. Know your weak spots and keep guard over your temptations and heart. Listen to your spiritual conscience and not your fleshly, sin-trained soul conscience.

Above all else, read the Scriptures daily and be in a spirit of prayer at all times, physically praying as well, whenever possible. A strong walk with Jesus will help you ride any storms of life that assail you. Learn to TRUST Him in everything you do. Jesus cares about every part of our lives; nothing is too insignificant to Him.

CHAPTER THREE

GOD'S PLANS A and B FOR OUR LIVES — Believers

God has a plan for each and every person in the world! He chose each of us from the very beginning before mankind was even created! Remember the Scripture that I shared earlier when God was speaking to Jeremiah?

He said, "Before I formed you in the womb I knew you...and before you were born..." Jeremiah 1:5

God knew each and every one of us before our conception and birth and knew exactly what our choices and actions would be!

We were known to God before our time and will continue to be known by God for eternity. Not one human being can die forever. When we die, our life for **eternity** will be determined by the choice we make here on earth. This is serious, *deadly* serious.

God does not want robots, so He has given each of us the right to decide for ourselves as to our future, with or without Him. He knows what our choices will be, even the bad ones. He will not stop us from making those choices.

Having said this, " EVERY person has the opportunity to participate in God's Plan A for life. He gave us freedom of choice. If we choose a different plan, we have nobody but ourselves to blame for the outcome.

That said, God does not abandon us because of our daily decisions. He keeps the "door" open for each person to change their minds **before they die**. That door shuts upon death and that person reaps the rewards or punishment they deserve, eternity in heaven with Jesus or eternity in the "lake of fire" with Satan and the other unbelievers. **Eternity is forever**, so your decision is extremely important. I cannot stress this point strongly enough!

God will give you every opportunity to ask Him for forgiveness, and NO SIN is too great that He will not forgive you. His desire is for all the people on earth to join Him in heaven for eternity. It is an important decision, the most important one you will ever make.

"Many 'Christians' think they are saved, hope they are saved, but still they doubt, wondering, "Am I really saved?" Our behaviour gives us a real reason to wonder. We are strong one day, weak the next, devoted one hour, flagging the next, believing, then unbelieving. Sound familiar?

Conventional wisdom draws a line through the middle of these fluctuations. Perform above this line, and enjoy God's acceptance; but dip below it, expect a rejection from heaven. Salvation then becomes a matter of timing and you just hope you die on an upswing. This is *not a good plan*! You need to understand *who you really are* in Jesus Christ! **He lives in us**; we are righteous in His sight. Learn to walk daily with Him, always seeking His forgiveness when it is needed. You will never be perfect here on earth, so learn to accept that fact; God already knows it, which is why He provided a means of salvation!

Jesus' language could not be stronger: "And I give them eternal life, and they shall **never,** ever [by any means] perish; and no one will ever snatch them out of My hand." John 10:28

The writer of Hebrews states, "I WILL NEVER [under any circumstances] DESERT YOU [nor give you up nor leave you without support, nor will I in any degree leave you helpless], NOR WILL I FORSAKE *or* LET YOU DOWN or RELAX MY HOLD ON YOU [assuredly not!"] Hebrews 13:5

6So we take comfort and are encouraged and confidently say, "THE LORD IS MY HELPER [in time of need], I W ILL NOT BE AFRAID. WHAT WILL MAN DO TO ME?"] Psalm 27:1; 118.6

8Jesus Christ is [eternally changeless, always] the same yesterday, today and forever.

You cannot love Jesus like He loves you until you accept the reality that, since you are in

Christt, His divine nature constitutes your own essence.

One thought to remember, even Adam would have gone to hell if he had not faithfully sacrificed lambs on a regular basis as God had commanded him when he was sent out from the garden.

The sacrifices in the Old Testament were made, looking forward, to the actual sacrifice of Jesus Christ, the Lamb of God, who died and rose again that God might be able to allow sinners saved by grace to enter heaven. *Without Jesus shedding His blood* on the cross to cover all our sins before a sinless Father, *we would all be condemned*, from Adam down to everyone who has existed.

There are many scriptures in the Bible to back up these statements. The first scripture is found in Genesis 3:14. The serpent had enticed Eve to sin first and she then convinced Adam to sin as well by eating the forbidden fruit. They received sentencing from God as follows:

14"The Lord said to the serpent, "Because you have done this, you are cursed more than all the cattle, and more than any animal of the field; on your belly you shall go, and just you shall eat dust all the days of your life.

15" And I will put enmity (open hostility) between you and the woman, and between your seed (offspring) and her Seed; He (Jesus) shall

[fatally] bruise your head, and you shall [only]
bruise His heel." Genesis 3:14-15

Eve's punishment was to be extreme pain in childbirth.
Adam's punishment affected everyone including all of creation!
The animals and birds would have their mouths shut and all
creation would be cursed until the day of salvation thousands
of years later. Yes, the animals and birds could speak in those
days.

One of the Dead Sea Scrolls, Jubilees 3:28 says, "And on
that day was closed the mouth of all beasts, and of cattle, and of
birds, and of whatever walks, and of whatever moves, so that
they could no longer speak: **for they had all spoken one with
another with one lip and with one tongue.**" Remember
Balaam's ass that spoke to him? He was not surprised; he knew
that in the past they did speak and will most likely speak again
when God lifts His curse on all creation.

Creation is still groaning, awaiting the lifting of God's
curse! The rest of the world is now waiting for the return of
Jesus to gather in all the believers. God had already provided a
way of salvation for sinners before sin happened. He knew they
would sin! (Genesis 3:15)

What is not mentioned here is the fact that we can
willingly take ourselves out of God's hands; example, joining
Satan as a witch, warlock, etc., declaring that God is no longer
your God. To die in this state would be fatal. That said, even
from the gates of hell, God will forgive even Satanists, IF they

ask God's genuine forgiveness BEFORE they die, turning their lives around to follow and worship Jesus. God loves His creation, including US. His will is for ALL of us to be with Him in heaven. It is **our** choice.

Using the information that you have now gathered about yourself, you will be able to determine, approximately, where you are regarding God's plan for your life. This will determine how it all affects your life going forward and will give you a guide on how to improve your "grade" until you reach God's Plan A for your life. You may already be there. If so, keep on doing what you are doing.

Only you will know when you are in <u>God's perfect will for you</u>. Do not let others dictate to you as to who you are in God. Trust God and go forward regardless of where you are at this point.

Plan A+ is heaven and Plan F is the lake of fire, both for all of eternity.

People who are believers in Jesus Christ and have accepted Him as their Lord and Savior are in the A's and B's and unbelievers are in the C's down to E's.

This is just a starting point and not an ending point. Do not be discouraged if you find yourself in the B's. You are still God's child, and He will help you get to your Plan A if you ask Him and work with Him on a daily basis. Ask the Holy Spirit to help you and give you guidance.

When an unbeliever accepts Jesus Christ and asks for His forgiveness, they are automatically "transplanted" into Plan B, all their sins are forgiven, and now it is time to go forward with Jesus. Where they go from there depends on how they develop their relationship with God and other believers. As you grow spiritually, your grade level increases, sometimes very rapidly. It all depends on you; only you will know where you are on this scale. You will never be alone, for the Holy Spirit will be with you to guide and to help you if you will let Him. Your roots will grow stronger and healthier as you develop spiritually.

When Jesus returned into heaven after His resurrection, He sent the Holy Spirit to all the believers to teach and comfort them in His absence. Just before Jesus went back up into heaven after His resurrection, he spoke to all of His followers who were present:

"...But you will receive power and ability when the Holy Spirit comes upon you; and you will be My witnesses...even to the ends of the earth." Acts 1:8

Also, In John 14:16 Jesus says, "And I will ask the Father, and He will give you another Helper (Comforter, Advocate, Intercessor — Counselor, Strengthener, Standby), to be with you forever—

[17]the Spirit of Truth, whom the world
cannot receive [and take to its heart] because it
does not see Him or know Him, *but* you know
Him because He (the Holy Spirit) remains with
you *continually* and will be in you.
[18]I will not leave you as orphans
[comfortless, bereaved, and helpless]; I will come
[back] to you.
[19]After a little while the world will no longer
see me, but you will see Me; because I live, you will
live also.
[20]On that day [when that time comes] you
will know for yourselves that I am in My Father,
and you *are* in Me, and I *am* in you.
[21]The person who has My commandments
and keeps them is the one who [really] loves Me,
and whoever [really] loves Me will be loved by My
Father, and I will love him and reveal Myself to
him [I will make Myself real to him]."

The goal for all believers is to get in the A's. Plan A+ is heaven with Jesus for eternity.

The **higher our "grade is," the closer our relationship with God.** That is God's Plan A for our lives. Plan A minus means we may need to get even closer to God than we are. This does **not** refer to what we are doing, what ministry we are in and what great things we have accomplished for God. It is the condition of our heart!

The other things follow naturally for some and different for others. We cannot all do the same things. We must each find out God's purposes for our lives that show to others and to ourselves that we are indeed children of God.

Just living our daily lives can be God's will for some of us; He looks on the condition of our heart and that is where we have our close relationship with God.

It will look, outwardly, very different from those in full time ministries, but we can be in Plan A in our daily lives. The secret is to be in God's will at all times.

The next question is, "How do we do that and how do we know that we are in His will?"

This is a loaded question and very difficult to answer because every single person is unique in God's eyes and only God really knows where we are in our spiritual growth.

We will never be perfect or sinless as long as we are on this earth. However, God has a plan for us and it is up to us to seek Him and get His wisdom and strength for our daily lives. Even Apostle Paul despaired of his status from time to time. Put yourself into Paul's shoes and listen to what he said many long years ago. Perhaps it will sound familiar with what you are experiencing.

¹⁴"We know that the Law is spiritual, but I

am *a creature* of the flesh [worldly, self-reliant—
carnal and unspiritual], sold into slavery to sin
[and serving under its control].

¹⁵For I do not understand my own actions
[I am baffled and bewildered by them]. I do not
practice what I want to *do*, but I am doing the
very thing I hate [and yielding to my human
nature, my worldliness—my sinful capacity].

¹⁶Now if I *habitually* do what I do not
want to do, [that means] I agree with the Law,
confessing that it is good (morally excellent).

¹⁷So now [if that is the case, then] it is no
longer I who do it [the disobedient thing which I
despise], but the sin [nature] which lives in me.

¹⁸For I know that nothing good lives in
me, that is, in my flesh [my human nature, my
worldliness—my sinful capacity]. For the
willingness [to do good] is present in me, but
the doing of good is not.

**¹⁹For the good that I want to do, I do not
do, but I practice the very evil that I do not want.**

²⁰But if I am doing the very thing that I do
not want to do, I am no longer the one doing it
[that is, it is not me that acts], but the sin [nature]
which lives in me.

²¹So I find it to be the law [of my inner
self], that evil is present in me, the one who wants
to do good.

²²For I joyfully delight in the law of God in
my inner self [with my new nature],

[23]but I see a different law and rule of action
in the members of my body [in its appetites and
desires], waging war against the law of my mind
and subduing me and making me a prisoner of
the law of sin which is within my members.

[24]Wretched *and* miserable man that I am!
Who will [rescue me and] and set me free from
this body of death [this corrupt, mortal
existence]?

[25]Thanks be to God [for my deliverance]
through Jesus Christ our Lord! So, then, on the
one hand I myself with my mind serve the law of
God, but on the other, with my flesh [my human
nature, my worldliness, my sinful capacity—I
serve] the law of sin." Romans 7:14-25

Is Paul saying that he is no good, that he is evil or that he
is living in sin?

No. He is saying that there is something dwelling in him
which is no good, but it is not him! Just because we have
Satan's spear jabbing into our conscience does not make us evil.
It means we are being attacked by something evil, the spear.

Satan bombards believers all the time, sometimes with
many "bullets" and sometimes with a "spear." He tries to fool
us into believing things we should not believe. He works on our
conscience to prevent it from protecting us from his attacks.

If Apostle Paul had all these struggles with himself, how much more must most of the rest of us struggle with ourselves in the same way. I put in the first part of the passage of Apostle Paul's struggles for a purpose! You can read the rest of the chapter to continue on with his message on your own. It is ALL good.

Using the information about yourself that you gleaned from the earlier pages of this book, you will begin to get a picture of what **you** are, what all of us REALLY are in our physical realm, our soul realm and our spiritual realm. We are tripartite in nature, and we are eternal in nature. What does all this mean to us, here and now, and how does it help us to deal with our lives?

If you are an unbeliever or you are unsure of your status in God, I would recommend that you read Section A – God's Plan for Your Life, at the back of this book before continuing this study, if you have not already done so. It is short, but it will give you a better understanding of what we are discussing in the next pages.

We will discuss the physical characteristics of our mortal bodies and soul first as this will give you a better understanding of the spiritual realm in your life. Apostle Paul talks about both the mortal body and the spiritual one in the scripture passage given above.

OUR SPIRIT IS ETERNAL
WE ARE A TRIPARTITE BEING

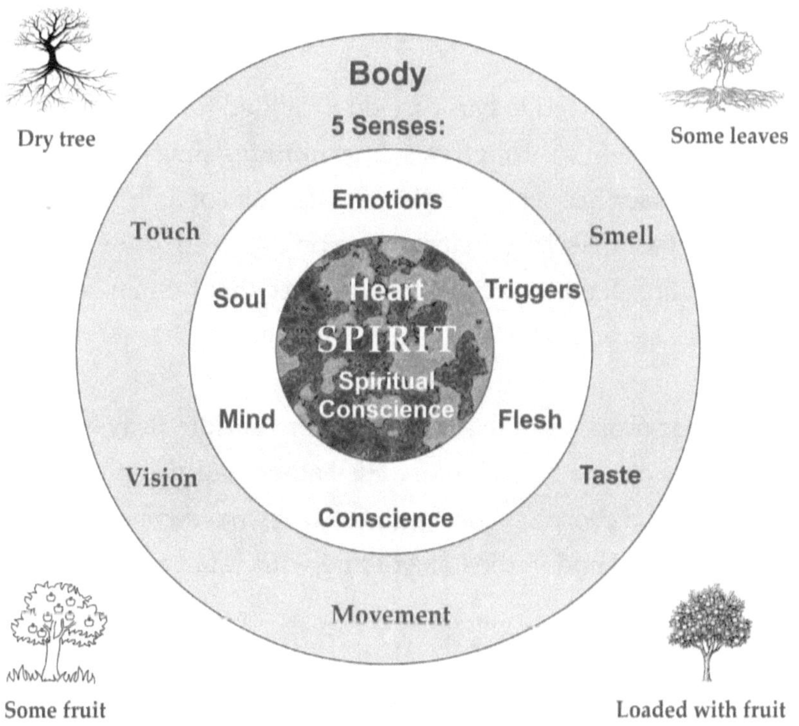

We have a mortal, physical *body*, which includes our five senses: touch and feel, vision, movement, smell and taste. We have a *soul* that consists of our mind, our conscience, emotions, triggers and flesh; we have a *spirit* which is eternal and also *acts as our protection against sinning*, our spiritual conscience. Our physical body will be replaced once we are in heaven. God does not explain what our body will be like...yet.

At creation God breathed life into our bodies and soul and imparted part of Himself, eternal life, into our spirits. Our spirits are a part of God, thus making our spirits eternal.

Animals have souls, but not spirits. They were cursed at the time of the fall of Adam and Eve. All creation was cursed at that time.

As I referred to earlier, God provided for the redemption of human beings through sacrifices until the time of the ultimate sacrifice when God's Son was born of a virgin and ended His career as a final sacrifice on the cross. Jesus took upon Himself all the sins of the world so that human beings could be saved and live for eternity in heaven.

He arose from the dead and went back to heaven to intercede on our behalf before His Father. Sadly, not all human beings have chosen to join Jesus, but they have gone their own way and will end in the Lake of Fire with Satan at the end of times.

Through salvation we become righteous in the eyes of God, the Father, as He looks at us through the shed blood of His only begotten Son. Our old nature **dies** on the cross with Jesus. However, even though we become righteous, we are not instantly made perfect in the eyes of God.

Because we are still very much human beings, we can and do still sin in the eyes of God. That does not mean we are lost every time we sin! Our sinful nature is dead! We are in the process of **being saved**. How can this be?

At the time of our salvation all of our past sins are washed away, and we are made as white as snow, righteous children of God. We exchanged our old nature for our new nature. This will be discussed in much more detail in the following pages.

****

Sanctification is the process
of becoming, in your behaviour,
what you already are in your destiny.

In Ephesians 5:8 to 12 we read, [8]"For once you were darkness, but now you are Light in the Lord; walk as children of Light [live as those who are native-born to the Light]

[9](for the fruit [the effect, the result] of the Light consists in all goodness and righteousness and truth),

[10]trying to learn [by experience] what is pleasing to the Lord [and letting your lifestyles be examples of what is acceptable to Him—your behaviour expressing gratitude to God for your salvation].

[11]Do not participate in the worthless *and* unproductive deeds of darkness, but instead expose them [by exemplifying personal integrity, moral courage, and godly character];

[12]for it is disgraceful even to mention the things that such people practice in secret."

The rest of chapter 5 is excellent and it is well worth taking your time to read it! God's Word is the food for your soul and will help your spiritual growth better and faster than anything else you can do. You want your roots to go strong and long so that they can drink water from the river of life. God's Word will grow your roots very rapidly; add prayer and they will get even stronger, strong enough to see you through any "storm."

The **natural person's** actions, reactions, habits, memories and responses are all governed by the flesh (our natural mind), which gives sin its opportunity. We will struggle with feelings of inferiority, insecurity, inadequacy, guilt, worry and doubt.

The **soul** of the spiritual person also reflects a change, generated by spiritual birth. We now receive our impetus from the Spirit, not from the flesh. Our mind has been renewed and transformed. Our emotions are characterized by peace and joy instead of turmoil. We are now free to **choose not** to walk according to the flesh, but to walk according to the Spirit. As we exercise this choice, to live in the Spirit, our life will begin to bear the fruit of the Spirit.

The flesh is still present in the spiritual person, but we must responsibly crucify our flesh and its desires on a daily basis, dead to sin.

****

This description of a spiritual individual is
the ideal model of maturity toward which
we are all growing...our choice!

Our physical bodies are a temple of God that needs repairing. How is it damaged? By indulging in physical appetites at the whim of a sinful flesh when we should be crucifying our flesh, by conquering feelings of inferiority, insecurity, inadequacy, guilt, worry and doubt.

Most of us struggle with our behaviour because we are struggling with the belief aspect of our growth—**we are in Christ.**

****

When you think that you have your Spirit-filled walk
to perfection, it probably is not Spirit-filled anymore...
beware of pride!

****

What happens when we still sin?

God knows our heart, and He knows that we do the things we would not wish to do. Remember the words of Apostle Paul that you just read earlier. He said he does the things he does not wish to do, making him feel absolutely miserable and confused.

What should we do about our daily sins and the things we do that we do not really want to do? We need to take them to Jesus on a daily basis. Whenever we fail, we get up again, ask His divine forgiveness and go forward. We are only failures and unforgiven when we keep our sins and keep on sinning!

How many times must we do that? Seventy times seven was the answer Jesus gave to His disciples. In Matthew 18:20

55

and 21 Peter asks Jesus how many times he must forgive someone who sins against him and Jesus answers, "I say to you, not up to seven times but seventy times seven."

In other words no matter how much or how long we sin, He will always forgive us when we truly repent and ask for forgiveness. It is not our spiritual heart that sins, but our earthly CONSCIENCE that we still have while alive in our mortal bodies, that will warn us when we sin; but if we do not listen, it is **not** our spiritual heart that fails. It is a constant battle between our mortal conscience and our spiritual heart.

Our conscience is our protection, but when we ignore its warnings, we sin. Our spiritual heart does not quietly accept when our conscience is tempting us to do wrong, but rather it wars against our conscience for control of our lives. That is where the confusion and struggle enters our lives.

Our conscience says we can do it and get away with it; our spiritual heart says, "No way!" Sometimes the natural desires win and we sin, again and again. **It does not have to be such a terrible battle all the time!**

Apostle Paul found the answer, Jesus. The more we commune with Jesus and read the scriptures, the stronger our hearts will become. A heart that is strong and spiritually well will conquer a weak and struggling conscience.

However, the opposite can also happen. The more we give in to our conscience and deliberately do things we know we should not do, the weaker our conscience will become and our spiritual life will begin to falter, and we will fail more than we win. It is our own personal choice.

God does not make you walk in the Spirit; the devil cannot make you walk in the flesh, but he will try his best to entice you in that direction.

When I look around at the churches and believers in our world today, I cannot help but feel that most of us are in the B's somewhere, some B+ and some B-. It takes closeness with Jesus to get into the A's. All of us desire to be there, but **not all of us want to be there bad enough to put forth the effort** it takes to read the Scriptures and commune with Jesus on a daily basis.

Choose Jesus. Be faithful in communicating with Him and reading the Scriptures. Remember, the Scriptures are the food for our spirit! The key to a restful relationship with Jesus is to learn from Him and open yourself to His gentleness and humility.

****

Walking in the Spirit
is more a relationship than a regimen.
****

Develop a prayer life – a relationship with God...more than just thankfulness and needs.

If you find yourself in a fallen state as a believer, sometimes referred to as a backslider, all is not lost. Jesus will **always forgive you** and give you a clean and fresh heart to start all over again. Nourish your heart with the Scriptures and commune with Jesus continually!

You do not always have to be talking to Him but live in a spirit of communion, being fully aware of His presence with you at all times. You can just share something with Him or just think about Him from time to time.

Example: you love your spouse and children, but you cannot always be physically with them. However, you think about them, possibly "chat" with them when you are apart.

You do not stop loving them or thinking about them in the background when you are working or travelling apart from them. That is the way it is with Jesus. He is an integral part of the believer's life.

We cannot always be praying or talking with Him but we can have a "spirit of communion" with Him in the background at all times. We take our troubles to Him and share our blessings and thanks with Him. He is part of our daily living.

The stronger this bond becomes, the stronger our resistance will be against the weakened demands of our mortal soul. Our soul will become weaker and not tempt us as much. **Love conquers evil.**

We need to be filled with the spiritual love of God that becomes so strong that people notice and are drawn to us for help, advice and prayer. This is the goal for believers—being 100% in the "camp" of Jesus. He will see us through the hard times, regardless of what they are and how often they strike!

Our Jesus is Lord of Lords and King of Kings. He controls all the wealth of the world; all the riches of the world are His to give. He longs to share these riches with the believers and often does. We are His children and He knows our needs. He will take care of us when we do our part.

The main issue is learning to walk in harmony with our new nature. We do not become a Christian by acting like one.

We are not on a performance basis with God. We cannot change our nature by improving our behaviour. God must change our nature, give us a brand new self—the life of Christ in us. This is the grace you need to measure up to God's standards.

This is the difference between spirit-filled believers and those who are "acting" like believers.

In Matthew 5:20 Jesus says, "For I say to you that unless your righteousness (uprightness, moral essence) is more than that of the scribes and Pharisees, you will never enter the kingdom of heaven."

When we learn to put our entire **trust** in His hands, He promises **never** to forsake us, no matter how hard things appear to be. Remember Job! He lost everything he had, plus ten children, yet he remained true to God. He questioned God, and he agonized over the boils that covered his body, but he survived. God restored everything he lost and even gave him ten more children over the next few years. {There is mention of only one wife; I kind of feel sorry for her having to give birth to ten more children!}

God treats each one of us as if we were the only child He has. Remember the story of the shepherd. One sheep went missing; he left the other 99 sheep and went and found and rescued that one sheep. We are not sheep, so imagine how much more important each one of us is to God.

In Colossians 3:3 it says, "For you died [to this world], and your [new, real] life is hidden with Christ in God."

If we are struggling to "die" to sins, we have a problem. We cannot do that, for *believers are already "dead"* because we died on the cross with Jesus Christ when He was crucified for our sins! We arose again with Him at His resurrection!

This death is not something that God expects US to do; we cannot DO something that we already are! We are already "dead" in Christ. God's redemptive work has replaced our old self with an entirely new self, which was not there before our redemption. The new life which characterizes our new self is *the life of Jesus Christ implanted in us.*

Getting rid of our old self was God's responsibility. It is our responsibility to control our "faulty" conscience that can control our lives by telling us something is okay **when it is not okay**. We must render it inoperative, stop listening to its so-called logic that permits us to sin. Our conscience lies to us when we are not walking close to God. The stronger our walk with God, the more reliable our conscience will become.

Sometimes we "justify" our actions so that we can do something we know is not quite right. Our sin-trained minds need to be *renewed.

Apostle Paul explains this perfectly in Romans 12:3:
"And do not be conformed to this world
[any longer with its superficial values and
customs], but be "transformed *and* progressively
changed] by the *renewing of your mind** [focusing
on godly values and ethical attitudes], so that you
may prove [for yourselves] what the will of God is,
that which is good and acceptable and perfect [in
His plan and purpose for you].

The Bible tells us that He even has a new name for each of us once we get to heaven for eternity. We are to be the "bride" of His Son, Jesus. After the final resurrection of all the saints, there will be the wedding celebration of the church with

Jesus. We will live and remain with him in the New Jerusalem for eternity.

For a detailed description of all that I am referring to, read the Book of Revelation, the last book in the Bible.

While the Book of Revelation tells all that will happen at the end times, it also tells us about the new city of Jerusalem that will descend upon the earth where every believer will have his own glorious abode in the city. We will rule and reign forever with Jesus. How exciting will our lives be!

CHAPTER FOUR

PLAN C down to PLAN E – All unbelievers

ALL of us **must** be born again. How is that possible? In the Gospel of John we see the full answer.

A Pharisee named Nicodemus came to Jesus one night and said to Him, ²"Rabbi (Teacher), we know [without any doubt] that You have come from God as a teacher; for no one can do these signs [these wonders, these attesting miracles] that You do unless God is with him."

³Jesus answered him, "I assure you *and* most solemnly say to you, unless a person is born again [reborn from above—spiritually transformed, renewed, sanctified] he cannot [ever] see *and* experience the kingdom of God."

⁴Nicodemus said to Him, "How can a man be born when he is old? He cannot enter his mother's womb a second time and be born, can he?"

⁵Jesus answered, "I assure you and most solemnly say to you, unless one is born of water and the Spirit he cannot [ever] enter the kingdom of God.

⁶That which is born of the flesh is flesh [the physical is merely physical] and that which is born of the Spirit is spirit.

⁷Do not be surprised that I have told you, 'You must be born again [reborn from above— spiritually transformed, renewed, sanctified].'

⁸The wind blows where it wishes and you hear its sound, but you do not know where it is coming from and where it is going; so it is with everyone who is born of the Spirit."

⁹Nicodemus said to Him, "How can these things be *possible*?"

¹⁰Jesus replied, "You are the [great and well-known] teacher of Israel, and yet you do not know *nor* understand these things [from Scripture]?

¹¹I assure you *and* most solemnly say to you, we speak only of what we [absolutely] know and testify about what we have [actually] seen [as eyewitnesses]; and [still] you [reject our evidence and] do not accept our testimony.

¹²If I told you earthly things {that is, things that happen right here on earth] and you do not believe, how will you believe *and* trust Me if I tell you of heavenly things?

¹³No one has gone up into heaven, but there is One who came down from heaven, the Son of Man [Himself—whose home is in heaven].

¹⁴Just as Moses lifted up the [bronze] serpent in the desert [on a pole], so must the Son of Man be lifted up [on the cross],

¹⁵so that whoever believes will in Him have eternal life [after physical death, and will actually live forever].

There is much more to the answer that Jesus gave to Nicodemus. You can read the whole conversation in John 3:1-21.

This answer that Jesus gave is part of the Gospel of Jesus Christ and is used to lead new believers to Jesus Christ. Salvation is for all people, but they need to hear about it and understand it. That is part of the responsibility of all believers, new and old. This activity, plus searching the scriptures and praying, communicating with God, will grow your character and your spiritual life to a higher status.

To the degree that you build your relationship with God, to that degree will you rise in your Plan level with God. The more dedicated and faithful you are, the higher you go. Your goal should be to find your Plan A that God has in store for you. It takes time and faithfulness. Some get there faster than others, but this is not a competition. The only competition is within yourself, your desire to get closer to God and to hear from Him and the Holy Spirit on a daily basis.

Unbelievers are unbelievers. God desires that all unbelievers turn to Him and become believers. He has a Plan A available for all human beings, but it is your choice to turn your back on God and follow your own desires if that is what you want to do.

You will end your life after death in Hell and later in the Lake of Fire with Satan. That is not God's desire for any human being. You will be in the lower grades and die there unless you make a decision to ask Jesus to forgive your sins! Hell is not a good option!

No matter how wonderful an unbeliever is, an unbeliever can never get above C in their own strength. Even good people who are loved and do great works cannot earn their way into the upper Plans. Salvation cannot be earned by being good and doing good works. Salvation is free just for the asking. The cost? Give your life to Jesus Christ and follow Him. Leave behind your sinful lifestyles. Without Jesus Christ, you live in sin because all human beings are born in sin.

The book of Proverbs in the Old Testament of the Holy Bible gives many examples of what God considers to be sin...anything that goes against God's Divine nature!

The sad part about all of the above is the fact that "religious" people are not necessarily true believers. Being true to a religion will not get you into heaven, Plan A+.

There is only one route into heaven. Matthew 7:13-14 says:

[13]"Enter through the narrow gate. For wide is the gate and broad and easy to travel is the path that leads the way to destruction and eternal loss, and there are many who enter through it.

[14]"But small is the gate and narrow and difficult to travel is the path that leads the way to

[everlasting] life, and there are few who find it.
[See also in Deuteronomy 30:19; Jeremiah 21:8]

C+ is the highest plan that unbelievers can reach without knowing Jesus. Plan F is the worst of the worst and is for those who choose to reject Jesus and are already worshipping Satan in this life and are very evil.

All other people are spread out in between. According to their deeds they will be known. This gets some of them rewards on this earth but not in Hell after death. We cannot take anything into Hell with us. This is sad but we make our own decisions. When God is left out, there is nothing left for us but life with Satan in the Lake of Fire for eternity. Their good works will mean nothing there.

This is not about good works and earning our way to higher plans. It is all about getting closer to Jesus. Read our Bibles and pray every day and we will grow, grow, grow, like the little chorus the children sing in Sunday School. It does mean working on our faults, giving them to God and seeking His help so that we overcome them.

Now that **you** have figured out approximately where you are {or not} in Jesus Christ, it is time to share some of the things you need to do and will want to do in order to further your relationship with God. Our relationship with Jesus determines the outcome for everything that we do; without Him we can do nothing in our own strength.

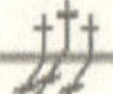

Apostle Peter tells us in I Peter 5:10:
"After you have suffered for a little while, the
God of all grace [who imparts His blessing and
favor], who called you to His *own* eternal glory
in Christ, will Himself complete, confirm,
strengthen, and establish you [making you
what you ought to be]."

Instead of focusing so hard on all the details of the
spiritual life, focus on trusting Jesus Christ, letting Him lead
you in the right direction.

CHAPTER FIVE

God's love for you is the great eternal constant
in the midst of all the inconsistencies
of your daily walk.

****

WALKING THE SPIRITUAL WALK

God's love and acceptance is unconditional. Do not trust your feelings alone. God loves you even as an imperfect person.

One of the secrets in achieving God's goal for each of us is learning to distinguish between a godly goal from a godly desire, there is a very real difference.

When I was young, my goal was to be a missionary in a foreign land. During a series of circumstances, that goal was never accomplished. Doors were shut and opened for me, but God had another plan! It was a godly desire, but it was not God's plan for my life. It was hard to give up a seemingly perfect godly desire to turn aside and follow God's plan for me.

I was disappointed, as I had it all planned! However, I have learned that God's plan for each of is always fulfilling, especially when you know that God is in control of your life. Later, my first husband, Gordon, and myself were planning to go to the "mission field" together. It never happened.

God shut door after door and after 17 years of married life, God took Gordon home to be with Him in glory.

I met my current husband, Peter, and for 42 years we have had the same desires, but God chose a different path for us; again I was "disappointed." Sometimes our lives seem to be completely "out of our control" as we follow Jesus in our walk, but it is also exciting.

At first we were disappointed and discouraged, but we are learning that the "mission field," for some of us, is to serve him **at home**! Our task and pleasure is to do the will of God to the best of our ability wherever we are!

*Spiritual growth and maturity result when
you believe the truth about who you are,
and then do what you are supposed to do
to renew your mind and walk in the Spirit.*

Our obedience to walk God's way and according to His plans for us has been hard and challenging, but good. We have never understood what He really wants for us, but we have put our trust in Him and it will remain there until we join Him in heaven. It is a marvellous comfort to know that we can trust Him with our lives and that He knows best what is good for each one of us.

*We need occasional mountaintop experiences,
but the fertile soil for growth is
in the valley of tribulations!*

A godly **goal** does not depend on people or circumstances beyond your ability to control. Only **you** can block a godly goal or render it uncertain or impossible for you. If you give control of your life to God unconditionally, He will open doors for you that would have been impossible for you from your perspective. Nothing is impossible for God! He is the God of the impossible!

****

God's plan for you is to "hang in" there and grow up!

****

Give God your *godly* **desire,** and seek **His** *godly goal* for your life. Sometimes, it will turn out to be just living a godly life in everyday circumstances with a one-on-one ministry. Learn to face disappointments of unmet desires. This is hard, but God will bless those who trust Him! My own personal life is a testimony to that fact.

When God does grant your desire, be thankful and humble. Avoid "spiritual pride" and give **God** the glory!

GETTING ON THE WRONG PATH?

Believing in what God has accomplished for us
and in who we are as a result of His grace
is the basis of Christian maturity.

When you base your self-worth on the success of your own personal plans, your life will be one long, emotional roller coaster ride. The only way to get off the roller coaster is to walk by faith according to the truth of God's Word. Make things right where needed and leave the rest to God.

Sometimes you need to do that moment by moment and day by day. Confess any sins to God and seek forgiveness from any individual you may have offended. Receive the forgiveness they offer and go forward once again on the right path.

Caution—your confession should only be to God and the individuals involved. *Your secret sins should be confessed only to God, not to any other person and not to your church body,* unless your sin has been against the whole church body.

Spiritual growth is NOT perfection; it is a walk in spiritual growth. None of us are perfect and never will be while we are here on earth.

Little knowledge of God and His Word...little faith;
Great knowledge of God and His Word...great faith!

Faith is active, not passive
Faith takes a stand
Faith makes a move
Faith speaks up

IMPORTANCE OF PRAYER

A strong and robust prayer life is basic to all Christian beliefs and activities. Without prayer we are as weak and helpless as new born babies, especially new Christians. Older Christians are not strong enough if their prayer life is weak. Most of us fail to pray as much as we should.

What is a "prayer life?"When you are praying, you are actually talking to God. Some pray directly to Jesus and since He is God as well, it does not matter too much. God the Father, God the Son (Jesus) and God the Holy Spirit are One, known as the Godhead. To know One is to know All. When Jesus taught His disciples the Lord's prayer, he had them pray to the Father.

At that time he was not yet resurrected and in His fullness as part of the Godhead. This is a separate study, so I will not get into the details in this book.

You can talk directly to Jesus at any time; He is omniscient and is with you at your side at all times. Jesus is the Groom and the believers will be His Bride when we all get to heaven.

GOD'S FINAL INVITATION—Revelation 22:16-17:

[16]"I, Jesus, have sent My angel to testify to you (to John, author of Revelation) *and* to give you assurance of these things for the churches. **I am**

the Root (the Source, the Life) and the **Offspring
of David, the radiant and bright Morning Star**.
[17]The [Holy] Spirit and the bride (the church,
believers) say, "Come." And let the one who is
thirsty come; let the one who wishes take *and*
drink the water of life without cost."

Jesus wants us to commune with Him all day long,
everywhere we go. This does not mean you have to actually
talk to Him all the time, but you need to invite Him to be with
you everywhere you go and talk to him from time to time and
share with Him your thanks, thoughts or needs whenever they
come up.

He will hear you and stay by your side as long as you
want Him there. When you neglect Him, He is still there but He
is standing "in the wings" waiting for you to invite Him back
into your life. I know I already said this, but it is so important, I
feel the need to repeat it!

**If you turn your back on Him, He will still be there, but
you will not have any communion with Him until you initiate
it.** The Holy Spirit will constantly be working on your heart's
door to get you to commune with Jesus and to search the
scriptures on a daily basis. The more you ignore Jesus and the
Holy Spirit, the colder and more carnal your heart will become,
and you will do things you should not be doing.

If this attitude is yours, you are somewhere in Plan B.
You need to search your heart and talk to the Holy Spirit and
Jesus and ask for forgiveness. God forgives us every time we

ask Him, no matter how bad or evil we have become. God is here on earth to help us, but He will never force us. It has to be our choice. **Jesus awaits you with His arms open!**

**You are never a failure as long
as you get back up and go again!**

Failure is when you fail and stay down, feeling sorry for yourself and making everyone around you miserable. Ask God's forgiveness, get up and go again. Keep in contact 24/7 with Jesus. He knows every one of us by name and loves us as if we were the only one there. Only God can do that, and He is God.

Romans 8:13: "—for if you are living according to the [impulses of the] flesh, you are going to die. But if [you are living] by the [power of the Holy] Spirit you are *habitually* putting to death the *sinful* deeds of the body, you will {really} live *forever*."

With a strong and healthy communion and prayer life we can move mountains and heal the sick. People will be drawn to you by the Holy Spirit and you will be able to minister one on one if not in a formal ministry somewhere.

Our neighbours are our mission field and the people on the streets of our town are part of our mission field. Keep your eyes open and your ears alert and allow God to lead you day by day. Very few of us have attained to this standard, but all Christians are "works in progress" as God leads and teaches us to love, honor and obey Him in all things.

SCRIPTURES FOR YOUR SPIRITUAL GROWTH:

Ephesians 2:5-6:

5"...even when we were [spiritually] dead *and* separated from Him because of our sins, He made us [spiritually] alive together with Christ (for by His grace—His undeserved favor and mercy—you have been saved from God's judgment).

6 "And he raised us up together with Him [when we believed], and seated us with Him in the heavenly *places*, [because we are] in Christ Jesus..."

Hebrews 13:5b: "...for He has said, I will never [under any circumstances] desert you [nor give you up nor leave you without support, nor will I in any degree leave you helpless], nor will I forsake or let you down or relax my hold on you [assuredly not]!"

Philippians 4:13: "I can do all things [which He has called me to do] through Him who strengthens and empowers me...[to fulfill His purpose—I am self-sufficient in Christ's sufficiency; I am ready for anything and equal to anything through Him who infuses me with inner strength and confident peace.]

GOD'S PLAN FOR YOUR LIFE...

ETERNAL LIFE

God loves you and wants you to experience His peace and life.
The Bible says:

"For God loved the world so much that he gave his only Son,
that everyone who believes in him may not die but have eternal
life. For God did not send his son into the world to be its judge,
but to be its Savior." John 3:16, 17

UNION WITH GOD--NOT SEPARATION

By nature man is separated from God. The Bible says:

> "...everyone has sinned and is far away from God's
> saving presence." Romans 3:23

GOD'S REMEDY IS THE CROSS

God's love bridges the gap of separation between God and you.
Jesus paid the penalty for your sins when He died on the cross
and rose from the grave. The Bible says:

> "Christ himself carried our sins in his body to the
> cross..." I Peter 2:24

MAN'S RESPONSE IS TO RECEIVE CHRIST

You cross the gap into God's family when you receive Christ as
your personal Savior. The Bible says:

> "Some, however, did receive him and believed in him;
> so he gave them the right to become God's children."
> John 1:12

PRAYER OF COMMITMENT

You can receive Christ right now by faith through prayer. God knows your heart and is not so concerned with your words as He is with your attitude. Prayer is talking with God. A sample prayer follows. If this prayer expresses the desire in your heart, then you can use it as your prayer right now:

> **"Lord Jesus, I know I am a sinner. I need you. I believe you died for my sins. Right now, I turn from my sins and open the door of my life and receive You as my Savior and Lord. Thank you for forgiving my sins and giving me eternal life. I give you control of my life. Make me the kind of person You want me to be. Amen."**

WHERE DO I GO FROM HERE?

If you have prayed this prayer, we would love to hear from you. Just click on Bible Maps and type in just your name and the country where you live. If you would like to be assigned a prayer partner, type "Yes" after your name and country. We will send you the name and country of your prayer partner. We can make it possible for you to communicate with your prayer partner if you wish. You could then provide specific needs for which you need prayer. If this is your desire, just type "Prayer Partner" in the e-mail.

You need to begin to grow in your relationship with Christ. You do this by talking to Him. Pray about everything. Pray specifically and pray honestly. God talks to you through the Bible; it is your spiritual food. Read it daily. Without spiritual food, you will become weak and sickly in your spiritual life.

Share your new life with other people. This is witnessing. This comes about as a natural result of growing spiritually.

Finally, find other believers who can help you and with whom you can fellowship. If possible, attend a Bible study class where you can ask questions and continue to grow into spiritual maturity.

FOLLOWING ARE SOME SCRIPTURES TO HELP YOU:

WHEN AFFLICTED:
>   Psalm 119:67, 71, 75
>   Psalm 34:19 -- God will deliver

WHEN ANXIOUS:
>   Philippians 4:6, 7 -- relieved through prayer
>   I Peter 5:7 -- God cares for you

WHEN DISCOURAGED:
>   Galatians 6:9 -- don't give up
>   Isaiah 41:10 -- God will strengthen and help

WHEN DOUBTING:
>   John 3:16 -- eternal life promised
>   I John 5:11-13 -- you can be sure

WHEN LONELY
>   Hebrews 13:5, 6 -- His presence promised
>   Psalm 16:11 -- joy in His presence

WHEN WORRIED:
>   Philippians 4:19 -- God will provide
>   John 5:14, 15 -- claim His promises
>   Hebrews 13:5, 6 – God will never forsake you

RECOMMENDED READING

1 Victory over the Darkness   by Neil T. Anderson
  Published by Regal Books

2 The Purpose Driven Life   by Rick Warren
  Published by Zondervan

3 The Holy Bible   Inspired Word of God

4 Abba's Child   Brennan Manning
  NAVPRESS

OTHER BOOKS BY THIS AUTHOR
Who is God? – His Name is Holy
Handbook and Study Guide
Includes many new and interesting facts

Conquering Your Fears
Handbook and Study Guide
Discusses many types of fears and
how to deal with them

Stable to Throne
Combined Gospels
All four Gospels have been skillfully
combined to make one complete story of
the life, death and resurrection of Jesus Christ

Understanding the End Times
Based on the Book of Revelation
What can we expect during the end time?

All the above books are available on Amazon
in several different countries. Check your
closest Amazon source for more information
on availability in your particular country.

http://www.biblemapsplus.com
Maps, Articles, Games and other Miscellaneous
Resources